The Bush-Ladies
In Their Own Words

The Bush Ladies In Their Own Words

Susanna Moodie

Catharine Parr Traill

Anne Langton

Anna Jameson

Molly Thom

The Bush-Ladies: In Their Own Words
first published 2000 by
Scirocco Drama
An imprint of J. Gordon Shillingford Publishing Inc.
©2000 Molly Thom

Scirocco Drama Series Editor: Glenda MacFarlane
Cover design by Doowah Design Inc.
Author photo by Monica McKenna
Cover photo by Brian Sytnyk/Vis-U-Tel
Production photo by Gordon King
Printed and bound in Canada

Thanks to Charmagne de Veer for lending a hand.

We acknowledge the financial assistance of the Manitoba Arts Council and
The Canada Council for the Arts for our publishing program.

Canadian Cataloguing in Publication Data

Thom, Molly
  The bush-ladies: in their own words
A play.
ISBN 1-896239-71-4

  I. Title.
PS8589.H45718B88 2000 C812'.6   C00-901160-9
PR9199.3.T4492B88 2000

For Mary Ann, Wendy, Elva and Meg

Acknowledgements

My thanks to the many friends and colleagues who have supported *The Bush-Ladies* in its long history. Especially, to Bush-Ladies past: Charlotte Hólmes, Margaret MacAulay, Joan Shaw, Rhona Buchan, Marie Bridget Dundon, Margaret Gobie, Rosalie Shackleton, Lindsay Empringham, Deborah Lambie, Sue Miner, Pamela Redfern, and Meg Hogarth who has been with the project from the beginning. To those who encouraged me to take the next step: Marion Gilsenan, Claire Hopkinson, Marti Maraden, Robert Missen, Carol Shields and Iris Turcott; to my indispensable travelling companion Margaret Edgar; to the Alumnae Theatre for setting it all in motion. And to audiences over the years who have shown so much interest in learning more about these ladies and their adventures in the backwoods.

About the Bush-Ladies

Susanna Moodie (1803-1885)
Roughing It in the Bush
The youngest daughter of a genteel but impoverished literary family from Suffolk, Susanna married "for inclination" the equally penniless J.W. Dunbar Moodie, a retired officer who played the flute, wrote poetry and had no fortune beyond his half-pay as an army officer. They emigrated to Canada in 1832, first occupying shanties on land near Port Hope and Cobourg, and then, in 1834, moving to an uncleared farm north of Peterborough near the home of Susanna's brother Samuel Strickland, and her sister Catharine Parr Traill. The Moodies did not prosper in the new land, and Susanna began adding to the family's meagre finances by contributing articles about her life in Canada to literary magazines. *Roughing It in the Bush*, describing the drama and disappointments of their first seven years in the backwoods, was published in London in 1852.

Catharine Parr Traill (1802-1899)
The Backwoods of Canada
In 1832 Susanna's sister Catharine married Thomas Traill, a brother-officer of John Moodie, and a month later they embarked for Canada to take up a military grant near Peterborough, where her brother Samuel had already established himself. She lived in the Peterborough-Rice Lake-Lakefield area until her death at the age of 97, the mother of nine children, an ardent botanist and the author of several books about her adopted country, including studies of wild flowers and several children's stories. *The Backwoods of Canada* was designed as a handbook for emigrating gentlewomen and was comprised of letter she had written to her mother and friends during her first three years in the country. It was published in London in 1836.

Anne Langton (1804-1893)

A Gentlewoman in Upper Canada

In 1837, at the age of 33, Anne Langton came to Canada with her father, mother and Aunt Alice to join her brother John who had settled on Sturgeon Lake. Before emigrating, she had partially earned her living as a painter of miniatures. She was devoted to art and music and was an indefatigable sketcher. She filled her days with the many tasks of a pioneer woman and with the teaching of the neighbourhood children. Her daily journals record her experiments with and eventual mastery of every household task from bread-baking to soap-making, candle-making, plastering, upholstery and sail-making, and present a vivid account of the day-to-day life of one family of settlers and a record of the growth of a community.

Anna Brownell Jameson (1794-1860)

Winter Studies and Summer Rambles in Canada

When she arrived in Canada, Anna Jameson was already a considerable literary figure, lionized in Europe as an intellectual, social critic and feminist. In 1825 she had married Robert Sympson Jameson, a young lawyer with a promising future, but the marriage was a stormy one. In 1833 he was appointed Attorney General of Upper Canada and, in midwinter 1836, Anna came to join him in Toronto to make a final separation arrangement for her hopeless marriage. As soon as the weather broke, she left Toronto to journey through the western part of the province—by steamer to Mackinaw, then 94 miles by "bateau" rowed by five French Canadian voyageurs to Sault Ste. Marie. There she embarked for the annual Indian conclave at Manitoulin Island, and continued by canoe down to Penetang, through Lake Simcoe, and back to Toronto, "having been absent on this wild expedition just two months." She published *Winter Studies and Summer Rambles* upon her return to Europe in 1838.

(Back row left-right) Mary Ann McDonald (Susanna Moodie), Meg Hogarth (Anna Jameson), (front row left-right) Wendy Springate (Catharine Parr Traill), and Elva Mai Hoover (Anne Langton) in the Toronto premiere of *The Bush-Ladies*.

Molly Thom

Molly Thom is a Toronto director, actor and theatre administrator. She has directed many plays by women writers, including the Toronto premieres of Carol Shields' *Thirteen Hands*, Caryl Churchill's *Fen*, Timberlake Wertenbaker's *The Love of the Nightingale* and Pam Gems' *Camille*. Other stage adaptations include Daisy Ashford's *The Young Visiters* and several plays in translation. As well, she is active as a dramaturge and director of new scripts, and is the founder of Toronto's New Ideas Festival which develops original writing for the stage.

Characters/Setting

Susannna Moodie, a writer
Catharine Parr Traill, her sister, a writer
Anne Langton, a miniaturist and journal-writer
Anna Brownell Jameson, a writer

Upper Canada 1832-1846

Production Note

The text is drawn verbatim from the writings of the four women. It is arranged as a series of conversations, stories or direct explanations in which the audience is always included as the fifth member of the group. Mrs. Jameson, especially in Act One, is an outsider, a visitor; although she sometimes joins in the conversation, she is frequently apart from the action, commenting to the audience on the experience of the three actual Bush-Ladies. As a reminder that these women all sat down after their day's work was done to record their experiences, they have notebooks which they refer to or write in from time to time. Mrs. Jameson in particular is an energetic recorder. The various Yankees may all be played by one actress or the roles may be distributed.

In Act One each of the Bush-Ladies has her own wooden packing crate, which serves as a seat and contains props—tea things, linen, books, silver, etc. The crates are also used to store away their travelling clothes. Mrs. Jameson has no crate, only a camp stool.

Production Credits

The Bush-Ladies was first produced by Beggarly Productions at the Studio, National Arts Centre, Ottawa (in association with the National Arts Centre English Theatre) on October 26, 1998 and on March 24, 1999 at Tarragon Theatre's Extra Space, Toronto with the following cast:

SUSANNA MOODIE .... Mary Ann McDonald
CATHARINE PARR TRAILL .... Wendy Springate
ANNE LANGTON .... Elva Mai Hoover
ANNA BROWNELL JAMESON .... Meg Hogarth

Directed by Molly Thom
Set and Properties designed by Mary Spyrakis
Lighting design by Alex Gazalé
Costume design by Margaret Spence
Sound design by Lawrence Beckwith
Dance Consultant: Beverley Miller
Associate Producer: Margaret Edgar
Stage Manager: Bill Brillinger

"Welcome, Welcome, Little Bark", words by Mrs. Moodie, music by J.W. Dunbar Moodie, arranged for *The Literary Garland*, Montreal. Reprinted in *Canadian Musical Heritage*, Volume 3, edited by Frederick A. Hall.

Introduction

I first began cutting and pasting the words of these four writers for a staged reading called *This Beggarly Wooden Country*—an account of life in the backwoods of Canada from four vantage points. It was arranged thematically since all the ladies wrote largely about the same things: the interminable forest, the appalling state of the roads, the reeking smoke-filled shanties, the cold, the insects. All spoke of loneliness, privation, the ague, the endless labour of clearing the land. What interested me were their four very distinct voices, and the collision of refined sensibilities with the rude raw wilderness.

This Beggarly Wooden Country was revived several times, and each time I rearranged it in what I hoped was a more fluid dramatic form. In 1997, I began yet another cut-and-paste, determined to move it beyond a miscellany of life in the backwoods to an examination of the women themselves—four women who set sail for the New World, their hearts full of hope and their carpet bags full of genteel accomplishments, including the writing of fine prose. With the new focus came a new title, *The Bush-Ladies*, and new questions: why did they come, what were their expectations, what did they find when they got here, and most important, who were these women and how did they endure?

Originally, the women existed in a sort of limbo of parallel experience and private reflection. But as I worked, the women seemed to want to interact, to inhabit the same space. In reality none of them (other than the two sisters) ever met, but here they were exchanging opinions and gossip and taking tea together. I became bolder in editing the text, building the piece like a patchwork quilt, playing with different rhythms and styles, the words cut and stitched together to construct conversations or disagreements, or to compress experience. Sometimes the anecdotes could be dramatized, sometimes the storytelling was so strong that the material had to stand alone.

Again and again, I went back to the originals, searching for the perfect line or the appropriate response to flesh out an exchange, or to find out more about the women. To tell their four personal stories using only the words they left us has been a sometimes frustrating but ultimately intriguing process of discovery. They are women of their time, their writing is not confessional or deeply introspective. There are gaps in what they reveal. But there is enough. There are hints. And for me, their words are what it's all about. The words connect us directly to their world, to the sensibilities and values of their time. And they tell us all we need to know about the women themselves.

Listen to Mrs. Jameson delivering herself of her absolute judgments: "A Canadian settler hates a tree"; "A woman who cannot perform for herself and others all household offices has no business here." Then this declamatory, opinionated person surprises us by her openness to new experience, shooting the rapids of the Sault with "giddy, breathless, delicious excitement." Look at the contrast between Susanna Moodie's romantic rhapsodizing over the grandeur of Quebec, "There frowns the cloud-capped mountain, and below, the cataract foams and thunders," with the heartfelt simplicity of "I loved the lonely lake with its magnificent belt of dark pines sighing in the breeze," and sense the journey she has come. She feels things passionately, she complains and rages, but she describes her domestic fiascos with a saving humour, her heroic exploits during the fire with a delicious sense of burlesque, and her Yankee neighbours with a sharp satirical eye. We know Mrs. Traill is precise and delicate and observant from her carefully detailed descriptions of logging and burning or the appearance of the Douro lily; she tells us with practical cheerfulness and new-found freedom, "we bush-ladies have a wholesome disregard of what Mr. and Mrs. So-and-So think or say," but we can hear now and then hints of strain and regret. Miss Langton catalogues her mastery of yet more arcane domestic accomplishments with mischievous, self-deprecating irony, and slyly gossips about the Dunsfords while attending to the serious work of educating "the untutored children of the forest."

"I must say, for all its roughness, I love Canada," says Mrs. Traill at the end of her book, and the others all concur, even Susanna. How did this happen? Where was the turning point, the experience or discovery that turned each woman's thoughts away from "home" and gave her a stake in her new country? They don't tell, so we have to guess. With Susanna it must be the opportunity to be published, to earn that first twenty-dollar bill which will reaffirm her identity as an author and help to maintain her family; with Catharine surely it is her discovery of native Canadian wildflowers; with Anne Langton the founding of her forest school.

Anna Jameson has her epiphany too. I think she discovered an unexpected side of her nature in shooting the rapids of the Sault and camping wild on the islands of Georgian Bay. She stayed in Canada a mere eight months, but everywhere she went her passionate curiosity was engaged, and she commented freely and forcefully on the position of women, the treatment of the Native population, the future of the country. In the play she functions as the traveller, the opinionated outsider. (Her introductory remarks about emigration are actually from Susanna Moodie, the only place where I have exchanged lines.)

Here they are, then, in their own words, these remarkable women: courageous, resilient, opinionated, hopeful, sometimes ridiculous, always supremely determined. I hope you will enjoy their company.

My thanks to four great ladies who embarked on this latest journey with me in a spirit of adventure and faith, and who, with their intelligence and wit, have added considerably to the development of the text.

Molly Thom
September, 2000

Act One

(The dense, interminable forest all around. Several wooden packing crates and bundles in the clearing. The women assemble as on the deck of a ship. MRS. TRAILL and MISS LANGTON settle on their crates, open their notebooks and begin to write. MRS. MOODIE gazes off. MRS. JAMESON, carrying campstool, carpet bag and notebook, observes.)

TRAILL: I received your last kind letter, my dearest mother, only a few hours before we set sail from Greenock. As you express a wish that I should give you a minute detail of our voyage, I shall take up my subject from the time of our embarkation. The day we set sail was a lovely one, and I remained on deck till night-fall. The following day we saw the last of the Hebrides, and before night lost sight of the north coast of Ireland. A wide expanse of water and sky is now our only prospect…

MOODIE: Dear husband! I am ashamed that my purpose is less firm, that my heart lingers so far behind yours. Like Lot's wife, I turn and look back and cling with all my strength to the land I am leaving.

TRAILL: I know full well the importance of the step I am taking—I am leaving the land of my birth, and will likely never again return. But hope is busy in my heart…

MOODIE: It is not the hardships of an emigrant's life I dread. It is the loss of the society in which I have moved, the want of congenial minds, of persons engaged in congenial pursuits—that makes me so reluctant to respond to my husband's call.

JAMESON: *(Introducing her to the audience.)* Susanna Moodie, a writer and the wife of a retired army officer. Her "dear husband" Moodie—poet, musician and gentleman—plans to take up farming near Cobourg.

Catharine Parr Traill, her sister and like her a writer, and the new bride of a retired officer. The Traills are coming to settle on wild land near Peterborough.

LANGTON: I begin to long greatly to see this future home of ours. "On Sturgeon Lake," my brother John writes, "you will find six settlers. Certainly this is not many, but then four of them have been at a University, one at a Military College, and the sixth, though boasting no such honours, has half a dozen silver spoons and a wife who plays the guitar!"

JAMESON: Miss Anne Langton, a painter of miniatures, sets sail with father, mother, and Aunt Alice to join her brother John on Sturgeon Lake. She begins a journal for family left behind.

LANGTON: I will give you a few hints in case you or any of yours cross the Atlantic. Bring a small mattress with you, for the aching of the bones when obliged to toss upon a hard, uneven surface for some days is no trifling inconvenience. In the next place, bring a few basin cloths, for one is apt to look upon one's wash-hand basin with perpetual mistrust.

TRAILL: Though we have been little more than a week on board, I confess I am getting weary of the voyage.

LANGTON: Do not be quite dependent on the ship's library for reading. There are odd volumes, pages torn out...

TRAILL: I have already made myself acquainted with all the

books worth reading in the ship's library. I have endured the horrors of *mal de mer*...

LANGTON: Our tea is neither good nor hot. The eggs are dubious. And go where you will, there is no quiet!

TRAILL: I sew, or pace the deck with my husband, and talk over plans for the future, which in all probability will never be realized.

MOODIE: To marry "for inclination"—what an act of imprudence in overpopulated England! We knew that emigration must be the result. And now there is the child...

TRAILL: Have I not a right to be cheerful and contented for the sake of my beloved partner? The change is not greater for me than for him; and if for his sake I have voluntarily left home, and friends, and country, shall I therefore sadden him by useless regrets?

MOODIE: It is a matter of necessity, not of choice. Provision must be made for the future. So, for your sake, dear husband, and for the sake of the infant, I will be reconciled. Hand-in-hand and heart-in-heart we will go forth to meet difficulties, and, by the help of God, to subdue them.

JAMESON: In 1830 the great tide of emigration flowed westward. Canada became the landmark for the rich in hope and poor in purse. Men who had been hopeless of supporting their families in comfort and independence in England thought that they had only to come out to Canada to make their fortunes!

LANGTON: *(Closes her journal and comes forward.)* They say that in Canada there are lands yielding 40 bushels to the acre!

TRAILL: And log houses can be raised—

BOTH: —in a single day!

MOODIE: Now, when one considers its salubrious climate...

LANGTON: ...its fertile soil...

TRAILL: ...its great water privileges...

MOODIE: ...its proximity to the mother country...

LANGTON: And last but not least, its almost total—

ALL: —exemption from taxation!

JAMESON: The infection became general. A Canada mania pervaded the middle ranks of British society; thousands and tens of thousands, for the space of three or four years, landed upon these shores. A large majority of the higher class were officers of the army and navy, with their families—a class perfectly unfitted by their habits and education for contending with the stern realities of emigrant life.

LANGTON: Mrs. Anna Brownell Jameson—

MOODIE: the celebrated authoress—

LANGTON: is coming to join her husband in Toronto.

MOODIE: She has lived abroad for some years.

JAMESON: I have heard it said that women who distinguish themselves in literature are almost universally women who have been disappointed in their best affections, and seek in this direction a sort of compensation.

TRAILL: She will not stay long...

MOODIE: ...just long enough to arrange a final separation from her husband.

LANGTON: He is the Attorney General of Upper Canada.

JAMESON: Surely it is dangerous, it is wicked, in these days to bring up women to be "happy wives and mothers;" as if for women there existed only one destiny—one hope, one blessing, one passion. We know that hundreds, that thousands of women are not happy wives and mothers—are never even wives or mothers at all. The cultivation of a woman's mind will not make her a less good, less happy wife and mother, but it will enable her to find contentment and independence when denied love and happiness.

TRAILL: Just one winter and one summer in Canada...

LANGTON: ...a mere eight months...

MOODIE: ...long enough to settle an allowance...

LANGTON: ...then travel all the way to Sault Ste Marie...

TRAILL: ...and back again.

JAMESON: Women need in these times *character* beyond everything else.

> (*Commotion and mounting excitement as they finally catch sight of land.*)

TRAILL: Today all is bustle on deck. Every glass is in requisition! "Land" is proclaimed from the look-out station!

MOODIE: The vessel has been nine weeks at sea...

TRAILL: Nothing can exceed the desire I feel to set my foot on Canadian shores.

MOODIE: —to put my foot upon the soil of the new world for the first time!

TRAILL: At ten last night, the lights of the city of Quebec were seen gleaming through the distance like a coronet of stars above the waters.

MOODIE: What an astonishing panorama! There frowns the cloud-capped mountain, and below, the cataract foams and thunders. Quebec, the city founded upon the rock! I leant upon the side of the vessel and cried like a child.

TRAILL: The captain has promised us a treat of new milk, white bread, and fruit!

MOODIE: The captain has promised a supply of fresh butter and bread!

TRAILL: The pilot says that at Quebec we shall find apples and fruit in plenty!

(The death bell tolls. The mood changes to shock and horror.)

MOODIE: At Quebec, the dreadful cholera raged within the walls of the city, and we were advised not to go on shore if we valued our lives.

TRAILL: The yellow flag is hoisted, and the invalids conveyed to the cholera-hospital.

MOODIE: Scarcely a person who visited the vessel was not in black. "It will be a miracle if you escape," we were told. "Hundreds of emigrants die daily."

TRAILL: In Montreal, the cholera had made awful ravages, and its devastating effects were to be seen in the darkened dwellings and the mourning habiliments of all classes. In some situations whole streets had been nearly depopulated.

MOODIE: The sullen toll of the death-bell, the exposure of ready-made coffins in the undertakers' windows, and the oft-recurring notice placarded on the walls, of funerals furnished at such and such a place, at cheapest rate and shortest notice, painfully reminded us, at every turning of the street, that death was everywhere.

TRAILL: In one house eleven persons died, in another seventeen; a little child of seven years old was the only creature left to tell the woeful tale.

(They gather up their carpet bags and move from crate to crate, perching momentarily, then rushing on, as they board one conveyance after another.)

MOODIE: At six the following morning, we took our places in the coach for Lachine, and left the spires of Montreal in the distance.

TRAILL: At Prescott we embarked on board a fine new steamboat—

MOODIE: —crowded with Irish immigrants, proceeding to Cobourg and Toronto. We passed Kingston at midnight..

LANGTON: At Rice Lake we caught another steamer to bring us to Peterborough before sunset.

TRAILL: Unfortunately, the steamer ran aground some four miles below the usual place of rendezvous.

LANGTON: It was certainly the most uncouth steam packet we had ever seen.

MOODIE: Noise and confusion till daybreak...

TRAILL: Imagine our situation, at ten o'clock at night, without knowing a single step of our road, put on shore to find the way to the distant town as best we could, or pass the night in the dark forest.

It was near midnight before we reached the door of the only inn. Wet, as well as weary.

JAMESON: To understand the full force of the scripture phrase, "desolate as a lodge in the wilderness", you should come here! The inn—the only one within a circuit of more than five-and-thirty miles presented the usual aspect of these forest inns; that is, a rude log hut, with one window and one room.

(LANGTON settles herself on the crate where MOODIE is about to sit.)

MOODIE: There is no such thing as privacy in this country!
             Think of it! A public sleeping room! —Men,
             women and children, only divided by a paltry cur-
             tain. Oh ye gods! Think of the snoring, squalling,
             grumbling, puffing! Think of the kicking, elbowing
             and crowding! The suffocating heat, the mosqui-
             toes with their infernal buzzing—

             (LANGTON graciously gives way.)

TRAILL: What would my English friends have said could
             they have seen the room in which my first night in
             Peterborough was passed? Truly it looked like a
             bird-cage rather than a bed-chamber—

MOODIE: *(Interrupting.)* And then, to appease the cravings of
             hunger, fat pork is served to you three times a day!
             Pork, morning, noon and night, swimming in its
             own grease!

TRAILL: The walls were of lath, unplastered and open so
             that the cool night breeze blew freshly through the
             bars, and I could see the white frothy water of the
             rapids dancing in the moonlight as I lay in my bed.
             It was a new experience, and wonderful to say, I
             slept soundly.

LANGTON: *(They move out to look at the wilderness.)* I well re-
             member the first look out in the morning. A waste
             wilderness of wood!... And the sticks and logs in
             every square yard of the little plain before us, to say
             nothing of "stumps"—

MOODIE: Oh, the stumps!

TRAILL: The stumps!

MOODIE: And beyond, as far as the eye can see, is the dense
             interminable forest.

LANGTON: Interminable...

TRAILL: Interminable...

LANGTON: It was the first bit of genuine "backwoods" I had seen.

JAMESON: The roads were throughout so execrably bad that no words can give you an idea of them. We often sank into mud-holes above the axle-tree; then over trunks of trees laid across swamps, called here corduroy roads, were my poor bones dislocated. A wheel here and there, or broken shaft lying by the wayside, told of former wrecks and disasters.

(They assemble to form a carriage, two seated in front, two standing behind, and bounce and lurch over the bumps.)

TRAILL: Over you go jolt, jolt, jolt, till every bone in your body feels as if it were being dislocated.

JAMESON: My hands were swelled and blistered by continually grasping, with all my strength, an iron bar in front of my vehicle, to prevent myself from being flung out, and my limbs ached woefully.

TRAILL: An experienced bush-traveller avoids many hard thumps by rising up... or clinging to the sides of his vehicle.

JAMESON: Deep holes and pools of rotted vegetable matter, mixed with water, black, bottomless sloughs of despond! The driver had often to dismount, and drag or lift the wagon over whole trunks of trees— or we sometimes sank into abysses, from which it is a wonder to me that we ever emerged. A natural question was—why did you not get out and walk?—Yes indeed! I only wish it had been possible. I set my teeth, screwed myself to my seat, and commended myself to Heaven.

LANGTON: *(Dismounting.)* It is marvellous how wood and iron hold together, to say nothing of bones!

TRAILL: Sometimes I laughed, because I would not cry.

(The driver, played by LANGTON or JAMESON, leads MOODIE aside.)

DRIVER: I guess—

MOODIE: —quoth our Yankee driver—

DRIVER: that at the bottom of this here swell, you'll find yourself to home.

MOODIE: And plunging into a short path cut through the wood, he pointed to a miserable hut.

DRIVER: 'Tis a smart location that, I wish you Britishers may enjoy it!

MOODIE: You must be mistaken; that is not a house, but a cattle shed, or pig-sty.

DRIVER: You were raised in the old country, I guess; you have much to learn, and more perhaps than you'll like to know, before the winter is over. *(He retires.)*

MOODIE: I was perfectly bewildered. I could only stare at the place, with my eyes swimming in tears.

(MOODIE is left gazing in dismay at her new home. LANGTON and TRAILL take off their bonnets and capes and open their crates to unpack a few precious possessions. NOTE: JAMESON never removes her bonnet.)

TRAILL: *(To the audience.)* The shanty is a sort of primitive hut in Canadian architecture, and is nothing more than a shed built of logs, the chinks between the round edges of the timbers being filled with mud, moss, and bits of wood. Sometimes the shanty has a window, sometimes only an open doorway, which admits the light and lets out the smoke. Nothing can be more comfortless than some of these shanties, reeking with smoke and dirt.

LANGTON: You cannot imagine how perfectly *comme il faut* rough log walls appear to us now; when we have got our striped green print up we shall feel as grand as King William amidst the damask hangings at Buckingham Palace. Hitherto I fancy we have more English elegancies about us than most of our neighbours, but the Dunsfords, I expect, will quite eclipse us, for they, it is said, are bringing a carriage out with them. I hope they do not forget to bring a good road too.

MOODIE: Without, pouring rain; within, a fireless hearth; a room with but one window, and that containing only one whole pane of glass; not an article of furniture to be seen, save an old pine-wood cradle. The rain poured in at the open door, beat in at the shattered window, and dropped upon our heads from the holes in the roof. And the wind blew keenly through a thousand apertures in the log walls.

TRAILL: *(Gently but firmly.)* Sister, in cases of emergency, it is folly to fold one's hands and sit down to bewail in abject terror: it is better to be up and doing.

(MOODIE refuses to be comforted.)

LANGTON: Confusion throughout! My brother John has engaged a plasterer from Peterborough, and now we really are going to have all our rooms finished. I expect we shall have much comfort when it is all over; our rooms will be warmer, although the sun will not shine so brightly through the walls as it used to do, and we shall not need to go around stuffing with cotton wool, and pasting brown paper over the holes as we did last winter. Moreover, every word spoken above-stairs will not be heard below-stairs, and vice versa, neither will it be necessary, when washing an upper room, to cover all the furniture in the room below it, etc.

MOODIE: *(Reluctantly takes off her bonnet and opens her crate.)* Matters are never so bad but that they may be worse.

MRS. JOE: These old country folks are so stiff, they must have everything nice or they fret.

MOODIE: Our new home is surrounded by odious Yankee squatters. They are as ignorant as savages.

MRS. JOE: Well, I guess you are fixin' here.

               (She starts looking through MOODIE's possessions. MOODIE intercepts her.)

MOODIE: In spite of wind and rain my little cabin is never free from the intrusion of Mrs. Joe and her children. Their house stands about a stone's throw from ours, and they come in without the least ceremony. Their visits are not visits of love.

               (MOODIE rescues another of her possessions.)

MRS. JOE: Old country folks are all fools, and that's the reason they get so easily sucked in, and be so soon wound up.

               (MRS. JOE carries off a silver spoon as a trophy.)

MOODIE: Men of independent fortune can live anywhere. If such prefer a life in the woods, to the woods let them go! But they will soon find out that they could have employed the means in their power in a far more profitable manner than in chopping down trees in the bush.

               (While the others are engaged in sorting through their household goods, MOODIE carefully folds a few baby clothes, then opens a book.)

JAMESON: A Canadian settler hates a tree, regards it as his natural enemy, as something to be destroyed, annihilated by all and any means.

TRAILL: The axe of the chopper relentlessly levels all before him. Man appears to contend with the trees of the forest as though they were his most obnoxious enemies; for he spares neither the young sapling in its greenness nor the ancient trunk in its lofty pride; he wages war against the forest with fire and steel.

LANGTON: The consumption of wood is awful. We burn, I think, on the average, about two trees per diem.

TRAILL: Some years hence the timbers that are now burned up will be regretted.

JAMESON: *(To the audience.)* There are two principal methods of killing trees in this country besides the quick, unfailing destruction of the axe; the first by setting fire to them, leaving the root uninjured to rot gradually or be grubbed up at leisure, or more generally, there remains a visible fragment of charred stump, painful to look upon; the second method is slower but even more effectual; a deep gash is cut through the bark into the stem, quite round the bole of the tree; this prevents the circulation of the vital juices, and by degrees the tree droops and dies. This is technically called "ringing" timber. Is not this like the two ways in which a woman's heart may be killed in this world of ours—by passion and by sorrow? But better far the swift fiery death than this "ringing", as they call it!

(Music under: a jig.)

TRAILL: My husband hired some Irish choppers to log up and clear a space for building our house upon. We, however, had to call the "bee," and provide everything necessary for the entertainment of our worthy hive.

LANGTON: These "bees" are getting a perfect nuisance; the period between seed-time and harvest is almost filled up with them.

TRAILL: *(Instructing the audience.)* Now you know that a "bee," in American language, signifies those friendly meetings of neighbours who assemble at your summons to raise the walls of your house, shanty, barn, or any other building: this is termed a "raising bee". Then there are logging bees, husking bees, chopping bees and quilting bees. *(LANGTON supplies "husking bees," "quilting bees.")*

MOODIE: They are noisy, riotous, drunken meetings, often terminating in violent quarrels, sometimes even in bloodshed. Accidents of the most serious nature occur, and very little work is done when we consider the number of hands employed, and the great consumption of food and liquor.

TRAILL: Sixteen of our neighbours cheerfully obeyed our summons—

MOODIE: Thirty-two men, gentle and simple, were invited to our logging bee.

TRAILL: The work went merrily on with the help of plenty of Canadian nectar—

MOODIE: Whiskey!

TRAILL: —the honey that our bees are solaced with.

MOODIE: Our men worked well until dinner-time, when, after washing in the lake, they all sat down to the rude board which I had prepared. Pea-soup, legs of pork, *venison, eel, and raspberry pies, garnished with plenty of potatoes, and whiskey to wash them down, besides a large iron kettle of tea.

TRAILL: *(Overlapping.)* *Some huge joints of salt pork, a peck of potatoes, with a rice-pudding, and a loaf as big as an enormous Cheshire cheese. We laughed, and called it a "picnic in the backwoods."

MOODIE: After the sun went down, the logging-band came back in to supper, while the vicious and the drunken stayed to brawl and fight. I was so tired with the noise, and heat, and fatigue of the day that

I went to bed. Mary, my girl, was soon forced to join me in my small bed-chamber, and my husband retired into the parlour with the few loggers who at that hour remained sober. The house rang with the sound of unhallowed revelry, profane songs, and blasphemous swearing. It would have been no hard task to imagine these miserable, degraded beings fiends instead of men.

TRAILL: Our bee was considered very well conducted in spite of the differences of rank. And so faithfully did our hive perform their tasks, that by night the outer walls of our house were raised.

MOODIE: And we were obliged to endure a second and a third repetition of this odious scene, before sixteen acres of land were rendered fit for our fall crop of wheat.

(MRS. JOE approaches.)

MRS. JOE: I've seen a good deal in my time; but I never saw a gentleman from the old country make a good Canadian farmer. The work is rough and hard, and they get out of humour with it, and leave it to their hired helps, and then all goes wrong. They are cheated on all sides, and in despair take to the whiskey bottle, and that fixes them. I tell you what it is; I give you just three years to spend your money and ruin yourself. And then your man'll be a confirmed drunkard, like the rest.

MOODIE: Oh ye dealers in wild lands—ye speculators in the folly and credulity of your fellow-men—what a mass of misery and misrepresentation have ye not to answer for! You had your acres to sell, and what to you were the worn-down frames and broken hearts of the infatuated purchasers? The Backwoods of Canada!

(The women gather to discuss the inconveniences and privations of bush life; LANGTON produces

tea from one of the crates. This is an outdoor tea party; the women perch uncomfortably on the crates or wander about the forest. Much swatting of insects.)

TRAILL: The weather is now very warm—oppressively so. We can scarcely endure the heat of the cooking-stove in the kitchen. The insects are already beginning to be troublesome, particularly the black flies—a wicked-looking fly, with black body and white legs and wings.

LANGTON: The blood is sometimes streaming from you in various directions before you are aware that you are much bitten. You would not readily imagine the amount of resolution it requires to sit still making a sketch when the flies are bad. And the mosquitoes will bite through anything!

JAMESON: Observe, that a mosquito does not sting like a wasp, or a gad-fly; he has a long proboscis like an awl, with which he bores your veins, and pumps the life-blood out of you, leaving venom and fever behind.

LANGTON: Next to the biters, our greatest insect pests are crickets. They are everywhere. I find they have been feasting lately on my shoeleather!

TRAILL: Besides the crickets, we are pestered by large black ants that gallop about eating up sugar preserves, cakes, anything nice they can gain access to. These insects are three times the size of the black ants of Britain, and have a most voracious appetite.

LANGTON: Beyond these we have nothing to complain of—in the insect way.

JAMESON: The want of good servants is a more serious evil. Almost all are of the lower class of Irish emigrants, in general honest, warm-hearted and willing; but never having seen anything but want, dirt, and reckless misery at home, they are not the most eligible persons to trust with the cleanliness and comfort of one's household.

LANGTON: The new girl will not do. I never, I think, saw one so thoroughly useless. She is inconceivable and indescribable. We continue, however, to like her, and therefore must consider ourselves comparatively well off.

MOODIE: They can live without you, and they well know that you cannot do without them. If you attempt to scold them for any slight omission or offence, you rouse into active operation all their new-found spirit of freedom. They turn upon you with a torrent of abuse; they demand their wages, and declare their intention of quitting you instantly. They tell you, with a high hand, that "they are as good as you; that they can get twenty better places by the morrow, and they don't care a snap for your anger." And away they bounce, leaving you to finish a large wash, or a heavy job of ironing, in the best way you can.

(MOODIE puts on her apron and prepares to work. TRAILL and LANGTON pack away the tea things and then put on their aprons.)

JAMESON: I have not often in my life met with contented and cheerful-minded women, but I never met with so many repining and discontented women as in Canada. I never met with one woman recently settled here, who considered herself happy in her new home.

MOODIE: Home! What emigrant ever regarded the country of his exile as his home? "I have got a letter from home!" "I have seen a friend from home!" "I dreamt last night that I was at home!" The heart acknowledges no other home than the land of its birth.

TRAILL: The men are in good spirits, and say they shall in a few years have many comforts about them that they never could have got at home; but they complain that their wives are always pining for home, and lamenting that ever they crossed the seas. They miss the little domestic comforts they have been used to enjoy; they regret the friends and relations they left in the old country; and they cannot endure the loneliness of the backwoods.

LANGTON: Women are very dependent here, and give a great deal of trouble; we feel our weakness more than anywhere else. I have sometimes thought, and I may as well say it, now that it is grumbling day— woman is a bit of a slave in this country.

(The following household chores sequence is performed as a stepdance of incessant activity and increasing exhaustion. The speaker pauses to deliver the text, as the dance continues around her. JAMESON is recording information in her notebook.)

CHORUS: Soap, candles, sugar
cheese, butter, dough
knit, spin, butcher
wash, iron, sew…

JAMESON: A woman who cannot perform for herself and others all household offices has no business here.

CHORUS: Soap, candles, sugar…

LANGTON: Candle-making, both moulds and dips, is the order of the day. I wish I could have an hour's conversation with a tallow-chandler to procure some hints concerning the business, as to the temperature of the room, temperature of the tallow, etc.

MOODIE: What can prevent a dip from being thicker at the bottom than at the top?

TRAILL:	And how near does the wick reach to the bottom of the candle?
CHORUS:	Soap, candles, sugar cheese, butter, dough…
MOODIE:	My first Canadian loaf. I felt quite proud as I placed it in the odd machine in which it was to be baked. I did not understand the method of baking in these ovens, and I put my unrisen loaf into a cold kettle, and heaped a large quantity of hot ashes above and below it.
TOM:	Oh, Mrs. Moodie! What is that horrid smell?
MOODIE:	Oh, Tom, it is the bread. Dear me, it is all burnt!
TOM:	And it smells as sour as vinegar.
MOODIE:	He stuck his knife into the loaf, and drew it forth covered with raw dough.
TOM:	Oh, Mrs Moodie, I hope you make better books than you do bread!
MOODIE:	For myself, I could have borne the severest infliction from the pen of the most formidable critic with more fortitude than I bore the cutting up of my first loaf of bread.
CHORUS:	Soap, candles, sugar cheese, butter, dough…
LANGTON:	Well! I had rather be a baker than a butcher. Yesterday, we cut up a quarter of beef. John was operator in chief, but the saw and cleaver were also wielded by female hands.
CHORUS:	Soap, candles, sugar cheese, butter, dough…
TRAILL:	Our society is mostly military or naval; so we are, of course, well acquainted with the rules of good breeding and polite life.

OTHERS: Ah, good breeding! Ah, polite life!

TRAILL: Yet here it is considered by no means derogatory to the wife of an officer or gentleman to assist in the work of the house, or to perform its entire duties, if occasion requires. In these matters we bush-ladies have a wholesome disregard of what Mr. and Mrs. So-and-So think or say.

CHORUS: Soap, candles, sugar
cheese, butter, dough...

LANGTON: Now, thanks to the increased facility of John's machine, I was pleased this morning after two days' work to weigh up 49 pounds of candles.

OTHERS: 49!

LANGTON: And I must tell you that Mary weighed up 52 pounds of nice fresh soap.

OTHERS: 52!

LANGTON: Soap-boiling approaches nearer to creating than anything I know. You put into your pot the veriest dirt and rubbish, and take out the most useful article.

OTHERS: Oh, so useful!

LANGTON: By the bye, the two elder ladies have been very busy today upholstering. I do not think any ladies on the lake have better-fitting garments than our two armchairs.

CHORUS: Soap, candles, sugar...

LANGTON: A few glover's needles would be a useful article to send us.

TRAILL: There are no tailors in the bush.

JAMESON: I have observed that really accomplished women, accustomed to what is called the best society, have more resources here, and manage better, than some women who have no claims to social distinction of any kind but whom I find lamenting over themselves as if they had been so many exiled princesses. Can you imagine the position of a fretful, frivolous woman, strong neither in mind nor frame, abandoned to her own resources in the wilds of Upper Canada? I do not believe you can imagine anything so pitiable, so ridiculous, and, to borrow the Canadian word, so "shiftless."

MOODIE: For a week I was alone, my good Scotch girl having left me to visit her father. Some small baby-articles were needed to be washed, and after making a great preparation, I determined to try my unskilled hand upon the operation. The fact is, I knew nothing about the task, and in a few minutes had rubbed the skin off my wrists. The door was open, and I did not perceive that I was watched by the cold, dark eyes of Mrs. Joe—

MRS. JOE: Well! I am glad to see you brought to work at last. I don't see, not I, why you, who are no better than me, should sit still all day, like a lady! You are so proud and grand. I s'pose you Britishers are not made of flesh and blood, like us. I hate you all; and I rejoice to see you at the washtub, and I wish that you may be brought down upon your knees to scrub the floors.

MOODIE: Ah, poverty! Thou art a hard taskmaster.

CHORUS: *(Forming a wheel.)*
Logging, burning, clearing
ploughing, sowing, reaping
logging, burning, clearing
ploughing, sowing, reaping...

MOODIE: Our man Jacob chopped eight acres during the winter, but these have to be burnt off and logged up before we can put in a crop of wheat.

TRAILL: We had a glorious burning this summer after the ground was logged up. All the large timbers are chopped into lengths and drawn together in heaps with oxen. The heaps are then set on fire; and a magnificent sight it is. When the ground is very dry the fire will run all over the fallow, consuming dried leaves, sticks and roots. Of a night the effect is very fine and fanciful, as the wind blows particles of burning fuel into the hollow pines and tall decaying stumps. Fiery columns, their bases hidden by dense wreaths of smoke, are seen in every direction, sending up showers of sparks that are whirled about like rockets and fire-wheels in the wind.

After the first burning, the brands are collected and drawn together again to be reburnt until the ground is perfectly free from all encumbrances—

MOODIE: Excepting the standing stumps…

LANGTON
& TRAILL: Oh the stumps!

MOODIE: …which rarely burn out and remain eye-sores for years.

TRAILL: The ashes are then scattered abroad, and the field fenced in with split timbers; and the great work of clearing is over.

CHORUS: Logging, burning, clearing…

MOODIE: The rain commenced about a week before the crop was fit for the sickle, and from that time until nearly the end of September was a mere succession of thunder showers; days of intense heat, succeeded by floods of rain. Our fine crop shared the fate of all other fine crops in the country; it was totally spoiled.

And now Jacob—the faithful, good Jacob—is obliged to leave us, for we can no longer pay his wages. Debt and misfortunes crowd upon us from every side.

(*OLD YANKEE WOMAN approaches.*)

Y.WOMAN: And what brought you out to this poor country—you who are no more fit for it than I am to be a fine lady?

MOODIE: The promise of a large grant of land, and the false statements we heard regarding it.

Y.WOMAN: Do you like the country?

MOODIE: No; and I fear I never shall.

Y.WOMAN: I thought not. For the drop is always on your cheek, the children tell me, and those young 'uns have keen eyes. Now, take my advice. Go home while your money lasts; the longer you remain in Canada the less you will like it, and when your money is all spent, you will be like a bird in a cage; you may beat your wings against the bars, but you can't get out.

MOODIE: Home! If only I could go home. "Home!" I repeat it waking a thousand times a day, and my last prayer before I sink to sleep is still "Home! Oh that I could return, if only to die at home!"

TRAILL: Susanna, when things come to the worst, they generally mend.

MOODIE: Our ready money is exhausted. We cannot hire. There is no help for it.

I had a hard struggle with my pride before I would consent to render the least assistance on the farm—to work in the fields—but reflection convinced me that I was wrong—that Providence has placed me in a situation where I am called upon to work—that it is my duty to exert myself to the utmost to assist my husband and help to maintain my family.

We have found that manual toil, however distasteful to those unaccustomed to it, is not after all such a dreadful hardship; and I have contemplated a well-hoed ridge of potatoes on that bush farm with as much delight as in years long past I had experienced in examining a fine painting in some well-appointed drawing room.

TRAILL: My husband has turned his sword into a ploughshare and his lance into a sickle; and if he be seen ploughing among the stumps in his own field, or chopping trees on his own land, no one thinks less of his dignity, or considers him less of a gentleman, than when he appeared upon parade in all the pride of military etiquette, with sash, sword and epaulette. Surely this is as it should be in a country where independence is inseparable from industry; and for this I prize it.

JAMESON: This is the land of hope, of faith, ay, and of charity, for those who have not all three had better not come here; with them they may, by strength of their own right hand and trusting heart, achieve miracles.

CHORUS: Our fate is seal'd! 'Tis now in vain to sigh
            For home, or friends, or country left behind.
            Come dry those tears, and lift the downcast eye
            To the high heaven of hope, and be resign'd;
            Wisdom and time will justify the deed,
            The eye will cease to weep, the heart to bleed.

            (*The depth of winter. The women are trying to keep warm.*)

LANGTON: My mother accuses me of not wrapping up. What do you think? At the present moment I am wearing two pairs of stockings, a pair of socks, a pair of shoes, and a pair of moccasins.

JAMESON: The cold is at this time so intense that the ink freezes while I write. A glass of water by my bedside, within a few feet of the hearth, is a solid mass of ice in the morning.

LANGTON: When Aunt Alice and I were pasting up the wind-holes, my mother reproved us, saying it was ridiculous for people to come to Canada and not be able to bear a breath of air. She is determined not to be soft.

MOODIE: In spite of all my boasted fortitude—and I think my powers of endurance have been tried to the utmost since my sojourn in this country—the rigour of the climate subdued my proud, independent English spirit, and I actually shamed my womanhood, and cried with the cold.

TRAILL: You say you fear the rigours of the Canadian winter will kill me. I never enjoyed better health!

MOODIE: The morning of the seventh was so intensely cold that everything liquid froze in the house. The wood for the fire was green, and it ignited too slowly to satisfy the shivering impatience of women and children. I vented mine in grumbling over the wretched fire, at which I in vain endeavoured to thaw frozen bread and to dress crying children.

I had hired a young Irish girl the day before, and she had never seen a stove until she came to our house. She was a good-natured creature, and she thought that she would see if she could make a good fire for us. Without saying one word about her intention, she slipped out, ran round to the woodyard, filled her lap with cedar chips and, not knowing the nature of the stove, filled it entirely with the light wood.

(The IRISH GIRL mimes filling the stove, etc.)

Before I had the least idea of my danger, I was aroused by the crackling and roaring of a large fire and a suffocating smell of burning soot. I opened the door to the parlour, and to my dismay found the stove red-hot from the front plate to the topmost pipe.

My first impulse was to plunge a blanket into cold water. This I thrust into the stove, and upon it I threw water until all was cool below. I then ran up to the loft, and, by exhausting all the water in the house, contrived to cool down the pipes. I then sent the girl out of doors to look at the roof. She quickly returned, stamping and tearing her hair, and making a variety of uncouth outcries, from which I gathered that the roof was in flames.

(The IRISH GIRL, wailing and wringing her hands.)

MOODIE: You must go for help! Run as fast as you can to my sister's, and fetch your master!

GIRL: And lave you, ma'arm, and the childher alone wid the burnin' house?

MOODIE: Yes, yes! Don't stay one moment.

GIRL: But I have no shoes, ma'arm, and the snow is so deep!

MOODIE: Put on your master's boots; make haste, or we shall be lost!

GIRL: *(Shrieking as she runs.)* Fire! Fire! Fire!

MOODIE: What should I save first? Bedding and clothing appeared the most essential, and I set to work to drag all that I could from my burning home. Large pieces of burning pine began to fall through the ceiling. The children I had kept under a large dresser, but it now appeared absolutely necessary to remove them. To expose the young, tender things to the direful cold was almost as bad as leaving them to the mercy of the fire. I emptied all the clothes out of a large chest of drawers, and dragged the drawers up the hill. These I lined with blankets, and placed a child in each one, covering it with bedding, giving to little Agnes charge of the baby to hold between her knees until help should arrive. Ah, how long it seemed coming!

(TRAILL and JAMESON, as MR. TRAILL and MR. MOODIE, come to the rescue. The IRISH GIRL, still wailing, brings up the rear.)

The moment my husband and brother-in-law entered the house, the latter exclaimed:

MR. TRAILL: Moodie, the house is gone! Save what you can of your winter stores and furniture.

MOODIE: Moodie thought differently. Prompt and energetic in danger, and possessing admirable presence of mind and coolness when others yield to agitation and despair, he sprang upon the burning loft!

MR. MOODIE: *(Springing onto a crate.)* Water!

MOODIE: Alas, there was none!

MR. MOODIE: Snow, then, snow! Hand me up pailfuls of snow!

(They form a bucket brigade.)

MOODIE: Oh it was bitter work filling those pails with frozen snow, but Mr. Traill and I worked as fast as we were able. More help had arrived, and the men were already cutting away the burning roof, flinging the flaming brands into the deep snow.

MR. TRAILL: Mrs. Moodie, have you any pickled meat?

MOODIE: Yes, we have!

MR. TRAILL: Well, then, fling the beef into the snow, and let us have the brine!

MOODIE: This was an admirable plan! Wherever the brine

wetted the shingles, the fire turned from it and concentrated into one spot. Our gallant friends soon managed to bring the fire under control before it destroyed the walls. *(Congratulations all round.)* Six men, without the aid of water, succeeded in saving a building which almost all had deemed past hope, showing how much can be done by persons working in union, without bustle and confusion, or running in each other's way. Beyond the damage done to the building, the loss of our potatoes and two sacks of flour, we had escaped in a manner almost miraculous.

(Music.)

Intermission.

Act Two

(To one side of the clearing there is a now a table and chairs, tea things, books and magazines. TRAILL and LANGTON are writing. MOODIE is darning, JAMESON reading a newspaper.)

TRAILL: Many thanks, dearest mother, for the box which arrived in August. I was charmed with the pretty caps and worked frocks sent for my baby; the little fellow looks delightful in his new robes. He grows fat and lively, and, as you may easily suppose, is the pride and delight of his foolish mother's heart.

LANGTON: Once more I have folded my paper to begin a new journal. Venetian blind-making, sail-making and stay-making have been my occupations this wet day, and my mother has been shoe-making.

TRAILL: Though at our first outset we experienced many disappointments, many unlooked-for expenses, and many annoying delays, on the whole we have been fortunate; our chief difficulties are now over, at least we hope so, and we trust soon to enjoy the comforts of a cleared farm.

MOODIE: Our affairs are now in such a desperate condition that it is impossible for them to be worse, and all chance of making anything by my writing has been abandoned. A year ago I was requested by an American author of great merit to contribute to the North American Review, published in Philadelphia. The hope of being the least service to my family cheered me to the task, and I contrived to write several articles after the children were asleep. But when I prepared to send the manuscripts to

Philadelphia, I found I was unable even to pay the postage of the heavy packets to the frontier.

LANGTON: Our breakfast table was graced this morning with eighteen newspapers, and, what was much better, with five English letters!

JAMESON: Apropos to newspapers—my table is covered with them. The number of newspapers circulated last year totaled more than 400,000 among a population of 370,000, of whom, perhaps, one in fifty can read;—this is pretty well.

MOODIE: Many a hard battle had we to fight with old prejudices, and many proud swellings of the heart to subdue, before we could feel the least interest in the land of our adoption, or look upon it as our home. All was new, strange, and distasteful to us.

(BETTY FYE heckles from the other side of the stage.)

BETTY: Ah, you Britishers, now don't you go to pass off your English airs on us. We are genuine Yankees, and think ourselves as good—yes, a great deal better than you.

MOODIE: The semi-barbarous Yankee squatters, by whom we were surrounded in our first settlement, detested us. They considered us proud, when we were only anxious not to give offence. We could neither lie nor cheat in our dealings with them; and they despised us for our ignorance in trading and our want of smartness.

BETTY: *(Loudly announcing.)* In this country we all live by borrowing. If you want anything, why just send and borrow from us!

MOODIE: Day after day I was tormented by this importunate creature; she borrowed of me tea, sugar, candles, starch, blueing, irons, pots, bowls—in short, every article in common domestic use—while it was with the utmost difficulty we could get them returned.

BETTY: Missus—I'm come for the kettle.

MOODIE: Whenever I saw her coming down the lane, I used involuntarily to exclaim: "Betty Fye! Betty Fye! Fie upon Betty Fye! The Lord deliver me from Betty Fye!"

BETTY: 'Tis deuced hard to outwit a Yankee!

(BETTY approaches.)

MOODIE: Well, Mrs. Fye, what do you want today?

BETTY: So many things that I scarce know where to begin. Ah, what a thing 'tis to be poor! First, I want you to lend me ten pounds of flour to make some Johnnie cakes.

MOODIE: I thought they were made of Indian meal?

BETTY: Yes, yes, when you've got the meal. I'm out of it, and this is a new fixing of my own invention. Lend me the flour, woman, and I'll bring you one of the cakes to taste.

MOODIE: Oh pray, don't trouble yourself. What next?

(I was anxious to see how far her impudence would go, and determined to affront her, if possible.)

BETTY: I want you to lend me a gown, and a pair of stockings. I have to go to Oswego to see my husband's sister, and I'd like to look decent.

MOODIE: Mrs. Fye, I never lend my clothes to anyone. If I lent them to you, I should never wear them again.

BETTY: So much the better for me! Well, I guess if you won't lend me the gown, you will let me have some black thread to quilt a petticoat, a quarter of a pound of tea, and some sugar; and I will bring them back as soon as I can.

MOODIE: I wonder when that will be. You owe me so many things already that it will cost you more than you imagine to repay me.

BETTY: Sure, you're not going to mention what's past; I can't owe you much. But I will let you off the tea and the sugar, if you will lend me a five dollar bill.

MOODIE: (This was too much for my patience longer to endure.)

Mrs. Fye, it surprises me that such proud people as you Americans should condescend to the meanness. of borrowing from those whom you affect to despise. Besides, as you never repay us for what you pretend to borrow, I look upon it as a system of robbery. If you would come honestly to me and say, "I want these things, I am too poor to buy them myself, and would be obliged to you to give them to me," I should then acknowledge you as a common beggar, and treat you accordingly; give or not give, as it suited my convenience. But you are spared even a debt of gratitude; for you well know that the many things which you have borrowed from me will be a debt owing to the Day of Judgment.

BETTY: 'Spose they are? You know what the Scripture saith, "It is more blessed to give than to receive."

MOODIE: Aye, there is an answer to that in the same Book which you doubtless have heard. "The wicked borroweth, and payeth not again."

BETTY: Wicked? Why you stuck-up, selfish, ignorant woman, you! May God roast yer stingy bleedin' carcass in all the fires of hell! *(Muttering as she goes.)* …stingy…selfish….ignorant…

MOODIE: And so she left me, and I never looked upon her face again.

         (Music.)

TRAILL: This is now the worst season of the year, just after the breaking up of the snow. Nothing but an ox-cart can travel along the roads...

MOODIE: Provisions are at their lowest ebb...

LANGTON: We are without fresh meat, the pork is done, we have no bacon...

MOODIE: Milk, bread and potatoes are now our only fare.

TRAILL: One time no pork is to be procured; another time there is a scarcity of flour. Then you must have recourse to a neighbour, if you have the good fortune to be near one, or fare the best you can on potatoes.

JAMESON: As yet I have seen no vegetables whatever *but* potatoes.

TRAILL: The potato is indeed a great blessing here; the poor man and his family who are without resources, without the potato must starve.

MOODIE: After bearing the want of animal food until our souls sickened, the different varieties of squirrels supplied us with pies, stews, and roasts.

LANGTON: We killed a porcupine here the other day, and ate it. It is said to resemble sucking-pig, but I thought it more like lamb.

MOODIE: Even the little chipmunk is palatable when nicely cooked.

LANGTON: By the bye, the Dunsfords laid in three hundredweight of butter for their winter supply, and consumed fifty pounds in three weeks. (*To the audience.*) You see, we gossip about our neighbours here as elsewhere.

> (*JAMESON gathers up her possessions and leaves the group.*)

JAMESON: Let but the spring come again, and I will take to myself wings and fly off to the west! To undertake such a journey alone is rash perhaps—I shall have no companion to give notice of my fate, should I be swamped in a bog, or eaten up by a bear, or scalped; but shall I leave this fine country without seeing anything of its great northern landscape?— And above all of its aboriginal inhabitants? The more I consider my project—wild though it be— the more I feel determined to persist.

TRAILL: You will have been surprised, and possibly distressed, by my long silence of several months.

MOODIE: Ague and lake fever had attacked our new settlement.

TRAILL: Few persons escape the second year without being afflicted by this weakening complaint.

MOODIE: The men in the shanty were all down with it, and my husband was confined to his bed, unable to raise hand or foot, and raving in the delirium of the fever. At Herriot's Falls, nine persons were stretched upon the floor of one log cabin, unable to help themselves or one another.

TRAILL: My dear husband, my servant, the poor babe, and myself, were all at one time confined to our beds.

LANGTON: Now the last woman about the place is on the sick list, and it is much more difficult to let women's work stand still than men's work. John had made up his mind that nothing could be done on the farm, but no bread! No butter! No clean clothes!— This is another matter.

MOODIE: After much difficulty, and only by offering enormous wages, I succeeded in procuring a nurse to attend upon me during my confinement. The woman had not been a day in the house before she was attacked by the same fever. In the midst of this confusion, and with my precious little Addie lying insensible on a pillow at the foot of my bed—expected every moment to breathe her last—on the night of the 26th of August the boy I had so ardently coveted was born. The next day my nurse was carried away upon her husband's back, and I was left to struggle through, in the best manner I could, with a sick husband, a sick child, and a newborn babe.

There was not a breath of air in our close, burning bed-closet. I was very ill, yet, for hours at a time. I had no friendly voice to cheer me, to proffer me a drink of cold water, or to attend to the poor babe. And worse, still worse, there was no one to help that pale, marble child who lay so cold and still, with "half-closed violet eyes," as if Death had already chilled her young heart. Bitter tears flowed continually over those young children. I had asked of Heaven a son, and there he lay, helpless by the side of his equally helpless mother, who could not lift him in her arms or still his cries, while the other pale, fair angel no longer recognized my voice or was conscious of my presence. I felt I could almost resign the long and eagerly hoped-for boy, to win one more smile from that other sweet suffering creature. Often did I weep myself to sleep, and wake to weep again with renewed anguish.

LANGTON: They say there has not been such a year as this since the year 1827, when it was still worse. In some settlements there is nobody near to turn to, and the poor creatures have nothing to do but lie down, and let the fever take its course. One widow woman, living alone, was found by the neighbours, dead two or three days.

MOODIE: Late in the autumn the fever finally left us. God in his mercy had heard our prayers, and we were saved.

TRAILL: "Do not tell me of lakes and swamps as the cause of
             fevers and agues; look to your cellars". This was
             the observation of a blunt but experienced Yankee
             doctor, and I verily believe it was the cellar that
             was the cause of sickness in our house all the
             spring and summer. When the snow melted, this
             cellar became half full of water; the heat of the
             stoves in the kitchen and parlour caused a fermen-
             tation to take place in the stagnant fluid; the ma-
             laria arising from this mass of putrefying water
             and decaying vegetable matter affected us all, until
             we each in turn became unable to help each other.

                 (MOODIE produces a letter.)

MOODIE: What do you think! Here is a letter from a gentle-
             man requesting me to write for a magazine called
             The Literary Garland, just started in Montreal! With
             a promise to remunerate me for my labours.

TRAILL: Dear sister! This is surely the dawning of a brighter
             day.

MOODIE: I have written to the gentleman and frankly in-
             formed him how I am situated. In the most liberal
             manner, he has offered to pay the postage on all
             manuscripts to his office, and has left me to name
             my own terms of remuneration. *(She assembles her
             writing materials.)*

TRAILL: Here, then, we are established, having now some
             five-and-twenty acres cleared, and a nice house
             built. Very great is the change that a few years have
             effected in our situation. A number of highly re-
             spectable settlers have purchased land along the
             shores of these lakes, so that we no longer want
             society. A village has started up where formerly a
             thick pine-wood covered the ground; we have now
             within a short distance of us an excellent saw-mill,
             a grist-mill, and a store.

LANGTON: Our young men have decided to hold a ploughing

match—the first agricultural meeting ever held in this district. Four teams will compete for the prize, and I have prepared some handsome pink ribbon to mark the winner. A tent will be fixed on the hill for a cold supper—and afterwards there will be dancing in the barn.

TRAILL: I am never weary with strolling about, climbing the hills in every direction, to catch some new prospect or gather some new flowers. I have promised to collect some of the most singular of our native flowers for one of the Professors of Botany in the Edinburgh University. I have noticed some beautiful lichens with coral caps surmounting the grey foot-stalks, a variety of fungi with a hollow cup of the most splendid scarlet within and a pale fawn colour without...

MOODIE: Now I no longer retire to bed when the labours of the day are over. I sit up and write by a strange sort of candle that Jenny has manufactured out of pieces of old rags twisted together and dipped in pork lard and stuck in a bottle. The faithful old creature regards my writings with a jealous eye. "An', shure, it's killin' yerself you are entirely; scribblin' and scrabblin' when you should be in bed an' asleep." Jenny never could conceive the use of books.

LANGTON: I had two little girls for a lesson to-day. I have lately begun to teach them a little—about an hour three times a week; I hope they will get some good from me, for they have nearly two miles to come for their lesson. As yet we are not all perfect in our letters.

TRAILL: The hepatica is the first flower of the Canadian spring. The wood-cress, or as it is called by some, ginger-cress, is a pretty white cruciform flower, highly aromatic. A very beautiful plant of the lily tribe abounds both in our woods and clearings. For want of a better name I call it the Douro Lily.

LANGTON: More new scholars today, and now I think my
              number is up. My mother has taken one little scribe
              entirely under her care, and Aunt Alice hears the
              reading lesson; our boy Timothy is her pupil—not
              a remarkably bright one, I'm afraid.

TRAILL: I suppose our scientific botanists in Britain would
              consider me very impertinent in bestowing names
              on the flowers and plants I meet with in these wild
              woods: I can only say, I am glad to discover the
              Canadian or even the Indian names if I can, and
              where they fail I consider myself free to become
              their floral godmother, and give them names of my
              own choosing.

MOODIE: My first twenty-dollar bill! I actually shed tears of
              joy when I received it from Montreal. It was my
              own; I had earned it with my own hand; and it
              seemed to me the beginning of a future independ-
              ence for my family.

              (JAMESON advances.)

JAMESON: It was June, and I travelled, joyfully alone, by
              steamer and bateau and canoe to see the upper
              lakes. My blankets and night-gear being rolled up
              in a bundle, served for a seat, and I had a pillow at
              my back; and thus I reclined in the bottom of the
              canoe, as in a litter, very much at my ease. I had
              near me my cloak, umbrella, and parasol, my note-
              books and sketch-books, and a little compact bas-
              ket always by my side, containing eau de Cologne,
              and all those necessary luxuries which might be
              wanted in a moment. We started off in swift and
              gallant style, looking grand and official, with the
              British flag floating at our stern.

LANGTON: I daresay our lakes, waterfalls, rapids, canoes, for-
              ests, Indian encampments, sound very well to you;
              nevertheless I assure you there cannot well be a
              more unpoetical and anti-romantic existence than
              ours.

JAMESON: At Sault Ste Marie, I lingered for a while looking over the rapids, and watching with a mixture of admiration and terror several little canoes which were fishing in the midst of the boiling surge, dancing and popping about like corks. One man (or woman more commonly) sits in the stern and steers with a paddle; the fisher places himself upright on the prow, balancing a long pole with both hands, at the end of which is a scoop-net. This he every minute dips into the water, bringing up at each dip a fish or two. I never saw anything like these Indians!

I have been given such a vivid idea of the delight of coming down the cataract in a canoe that I am half resolved to attempt it... It must be a glorious sensation. The more I looked upon those glancing, dancing rapids, the more resolute I grew to venture myself in the midst of them.

The canoe being ready, I went up to the top of the portage, and we launched into the river. In a minute we were within the verge of the rapids and down we went with a whirl and a splash!—the white surge leaping around me—over me. The Indian with astonishing dexterity kept the head of the canoe to the breakers, and somehow or other we danced through them. The passage between the rocks was sometimes not more than two feet in width, and we had to turn sharp angles—a touch of which would have sent us to destruction—but I can truly say, I had not even a momentary sensation of fear, but rather of giddy, breathless, delicious excitement. The whole affair, from the moment I entered the canoe till I reached the landing place, occupied seven minutes, and the distance is about three-quarters of a mile.

My Indians were enchanted with my exploit. They told me I was the first European female who had ever performed it, and assuredly I shall not be the last. I recommend it as an exercise before breakfast.

As for my Ne-engai, she laughed, clapped her hands, and embraced me several times. I was declared duly initiated, and adopted into the family by the name of "Wa-sah-ge wah-no-qua". It signifies "the bright foam" or more properly, with the feminine adjunct "qua", the "woman of the bright foam"; and by this name I am henceforth to be known among the Chippewas.

MOODIE: The Indians have set up their summer camp across the lake…

TRAILL: Old Peter's wife has been several times to see me, sometimes from curiosity, sometimes to barter her baskets and mats, sometimes to borrow "kettle to cook," which she is very punctual in returning.

MOODIE: Their honesty and love of truth are their finest traits. We meet them with confidence, and our dealings are always conducted with the strictest integrity.

TRAILL: When they come to visit, they now leave all their weapons, their rifles, tomahawks etc, outside the door, even if the weather be ever so wet, as they consider it impolite to enter a friendly dwelling armed.

MOODIE: The Indian is one of Nature's gentlemen—he never says or does a rude or vulgar thing.

TRAILL: We often listen with pleasure to them singing their hymns of a Sunday night. Under the milder influences of Christianity, their traits of cunning and warlike ferocity seem to have disappeared.

JAMESON: A war party of Indians, perhaps two or three hundred, dance their war dance, go out and burn a village, and bring back twenty or thirty scalps. They are savages and heathens. We Europeans fight a battle, leave fifty thousand dead or dying by inches on the field, and a hundred thousand to mourn them, desolate; but we are civilized and Christians. If our advantages of intellect and refinement are not to lead on to farther moral superiority, I prefer the Indians on the score of consistency; they are what they profess to be, and we are not what we profess to be. They profess to be warriors and hunters, and are so; we profess to be Christians, and civilized—are we so?

(An awkward moment. The candle is lighted. LANGTON pours tea. MOODIE returns to her writing.)

LANGTON: Another busy day! The Dunsford family is coming to visit. Five young ladies, all grown up! What a commotion they will make amongst us. There is to be a ball at Peterborough this week; two of the Miss Dunsfords are going down thirty miles to attend.

JAMESON: "There is no society in Toronto," is what I hear repeated all around me—even by those who compose the only society we have. "But," you will say, "what could be expected in a remote town, which forty years ago was an uninhabited swamp, and twenty years ago only began to exist?" I really do not know what I expected, but I will tell you what I did not expect. I did not expect to find here in this new capital of a new country, with the boundless forest within half a mile of us on almost every side—concentrated as it were the worst evils of our old and most artificial social system at home, with none of its advantages. Is there no one who will bring a few grains of truth to Toronto?

LANGTON: Now we have another great bustle in prospect—a Regatta! The word Regatta must vibrate on the air of these lakes some hundred and fifty times a day. Aunt Alice remarked, "I did say when we were coming to Canada, 'Well, there is one good thing in it, at least there will be no bazaars!'" Poor Aunt Alice! She finds us much further advanced in folly than she expected. We have not only bazaars, but regattas!

JAMESON: It is curious to see how quickly a new fashion, or a new folly is imported from the old country, and with what difficulty and delay a new idea finds its way into the heads of the people, or a new book into their hands.

LANGTON: I have been again trying to drive a little intelligence into the untutored children of the forest. I do not know what progress can be expected from children who say a lesson twice a week, and perhaps never look at a book at any other time.

JAMESON: It has been an ample source of ridicule that a house of parliament, of which many members cannot read, and many more cannot spell, should be zealous on the subject of education. But I feel no disposition to join in the ridicule.

LANGTON: I know the instruction I give goes a very small way indeed towards complete education. Most of my scholars have to begin from the a-b-c, and until a little reading is accomplished, I scarely think I can attempt anything beyond it. I begin to wish we had or could have something more regular in the way of a school.

JAMESON: At Niagara I asked for a bookseller's shop; there is not one in the town, but plenty of taverns. There is a duty of thirty per cent on books imported from the United States, and the expense of books imported from England adds at least as much to *their* price: but there is no duty on whiskey. There is, I fear, a good deal of drunkenness and profligacy.

TRAILL: Intemperance is too prevailing a vice among all ranks of people in this country; but I blush to say it belongs most decidedly to those that consider themselves among the better class of emigrants.

JAMESON: I find no means whatever of social amusement for any class, except that which the tavern affords; taverns consequently abound everywhere.

LANGTON: We all joined in a little tirade against Canada this morning, my mother's ground of complaint being the slovenly nature of its inhabitants. Poor country! It bears the blame of all the sins of the motley herd that inhabit it.

JAMESON: The mayor of Toronto complains of the increase of crime, and of poverty, and particularly of the increase of street beggars and juvenile depredators. Still, Toronto is a young place, and it must advance—it may become the thinking head and beating heart of a nation, great, wise, and happy; who knows?

TRAILL: One great want in this distant settlement, I mean the want of public worship on the Sabbath-day, promises to be speedily remedied. A subscription is about to be opened among the settlers for the erection of a small building which may answer the purpose of church and school-house.

LANGTON: I must get William to send us the notes of some good simple old psalm tunes. They will, I hope, be wanted soon for our new church. There is a book of such amongst my old music. I believe I oftener think of my music books than of my piano. Some dim recollection of an old favourite passes through my mind's ear, and I fancy I should like to see the notes.

(Music: phrase of an old psalm tune.)

TRAILL: My dear sister and her husband are comfortably settled in their new abode, and have a fine spot cleared and cropped. We often see them, and enjoy a chat of home—sweet, never-to-be-forgotten home; and cheat ourselves into the fond belief that at no very distant time we may again retrace its fertile fields and flowery dales.

LANGTON: It is four years since we landed at this place, and I
              now look upon the transactions of the neighbour-
              hood with more interest than I have felt for any
              neighbourhood I ever lived in. I never felt before
              that I was in the least likely to be permanently set-
              tled. Now, I think I may live and die where I am.
              There is so much happiness in having an object in
              life, and feeling yourself of real use to some one.

TRAILL: My husband is becoming more reconciled to the
              country, and I daily feel my attachment to it
              strengthening. The very stumps that appeared so
              odious, through long custom seem to lose some of
              their hideousness. Some century hence how differ-
              ent will this spot appear! I can picture it to my
              imagination with fertile fields and groves of trees
              planted by the hand of taste. All will be different.

LANGTON: When I take my morning walk, I look with pleasure
              and admiration at our verandah. The vines are up
              to the ceiling, and one of the rose-trees (a wild one)
              is nearly as high. When I think of what we were
              four years ago, our progress about the premises is
              wonderful, and repays us for all our care and
              painstaking.

MOODIE: These were the halcyon days of the bush. My hus-
              band had purchased a very light cedar canoe, to
              which he attached a keel and a sail; and most of our
              leisure hours were spent upon the water. The pure
              beauty of the Canadian water cast a magic spell
              upon our spirits. Every object was new to us. We
              felt as if we were the first discoverers of every
              beautiful flower and stately tree, and we gave
              names to fantastic rocks and fairy isles, and even
              composed airs about picturesque spots we floated
              past.

SONG: *Welcome, Welcome, Little Bark.*

              *(JAMESON blows out the candle and rises to ad-
              dress the audience.)*

JAMESON: There was a deep slumbrous calm all around. Daylight was just creeping up the sky, and some few stars yet out. We were now steering towards the south-east, where the great Manitoulin Island was dimly discerned. Towards the east, the atmosphere began to kindle with gradual light; and then, just there, where the lake and sky seemed flowing and glowing together like a bath of fire, we saw the huge black hull of a vessel, with masts and spars rising against the sky. One man was standing in her bows, with an immense oar, which he slowly pulled, walking backwards and forwards. We rowed up to the side, and hailed him— "What news? What news?"

And the answer was that William the Fourth was dead, and that Queen Victoria reigned in his place! We sat silent looking at each other, and even in that very moment the orb of the sun rose out of the lake, and poured its beams full in our dazzled eyes.

Many thoughts came into my mind—some tears too into my eyes—not certainly for that dead King, but for that living Queen, so young and fair—

As many hopes hang on that noble head
As there hang blossoms on the boughs in May.

And what will become of *them*?—of *her*! Even here, in this new world of woods and waters, amid these remote wilds, her power reaches and her sovereignty is acknowledged.

And what a fair heritage is this which has fallen to her! A land young like herself—a land of hopes— and fair, most fair! Does she know—does she care anything about it? —While hearts are beating warm for her, and voices bless her, and hands are stretched out towards her—even from these wild lake shores!

TRAILL: I must say, for all its roughness, I love Canada, and

am as happy in my humble log-house as if it were a
courtly hall or bower.

JAMESON: I wonder how it is that some of these gentry whom
I used to see in London, looking as though they
would give an empire for a new pleasure or a new
sensation, do not come here?

(Gathering up her possessions.) I have had *such* adventures and seen *such* strange things, as never yet
were rehearsed in prose or verse, and thinking it a
shame to keep these wonders only to make my
own hair stand on end, I am going to make a book
and print it forthwith.

*(She goes. TRAILL and LANGTON return to their
writing.)*

LANGTON: Mrs. Jameson can now return to Europe. She has
what she came for.

MOODIE: Her separation agreement...

TRAILL: And a suitable allowance.

LANGTON: And a book.

MOODIE: The potato crop was gathered in, and I had collected my store of dandelion-roots for our winter
coffee, when one day brought a letter to my husband from the Governor's secretary, offering him
the situation of sheriff of the district. My husband
looked upon it as a gift sent from heaven.

This last night of the old year has been ushered in
with furious storms of wind and snow, driving
through every crevice, and powdering the floor
until it rivals in whiteness the ground without.

This is the last night I will ever spend in the bush—
in the dear forest home which I have loved in spite
of all the hardships. It is the birthplace of my three
boys, the school of high resolve and energetic

action in which we have learned to meet calmly the ills of life. Every object has become endeared to me. I love the lonely lake, with its magnificent belt of dark pines sighing in the breeze; the cedar swamp, the summer home of my Indian friends; my own dear little garden, with its rugged snake-fence which I helped to place with my own hands.

Old Jenny is mad with excitement. "Ah! who would have thought, a year ago, misthress dear, that we should be going to town to live in a mansion? It is but yesterday that we were hoeing praties in the field."

Indeed, God has been very good to us.

TRAILL: The next time you send a parcel or box, do not forget to enclose flower-seeds, and the stones of plums, and pips of the best apples in the orchard. I should be grateful for a few nuts from our beautiful old nut trees. Dear old trees! And the seeds of our wild primrose and sweet violet. I long to introduce them in our meadows and gardens here.

LANGTON: Once more I take my leave of you, having now completed the twelfth journal. Times are somewhat changed since I commenced these scribblings. The announcement of John's engagement to Miss Lydia Dunsford has brought our year to a most joyful conclusion. And now I must tell you, I have determined to use my small legacy in the purchase of some land upon which to build a permanent schoolhouse. Two applications have been received for the post of master, and the neighbours have volunteered to give their services for the building. I will call the bee in the spring.

TRAILL: Surely this is a blessed country to which we have emigrated.

MOODIE: *(Joining them at the table.)* I often look back and laugh at the feelings with which I once regarded this noble country. My attachment to Canada is now so strong, that I cannot imagine anything which could induce me to leave. We may truly say, old things have passed away, all things have become new. *(MOODIE picks up her pen.)*

(Music: The Emblem of Canada, *played over as the lights slowly fade on the three women writing at the table.)*

The End